It's a Bug's World

It's a Bug's World

A Directory of Awesome Insects

By Paul Wray
Illustrated by Andy Hamilton

ELEMENT
CHILDREN'S BOOKS

SHAFTESBURY, DORSET . BOSTON, MASSACHUSETTS. MELBOURNE, VICTORIA

For Mum and Dad

First published in Great Britain in 1999 by
Element Children's Books
Shaftesbury, Dorset SP7 8BP

Published in the USA in 1999 by
Element Books, Inc.
160 North Washington Street,
Boston MA 02114

Published in Australia in 1999 by
Element Books and distributed by
Penguin Australia Limited,
487 Maroondah Highway, Ringwood,
Victoria 3134

Cover and inside design by b3.
Cover illustration by Tony Watson.
Printed and bound in Great Britain by
JW Arrowsmith Ltd, Bristol.

British Library Cataloguing in Publication data available.
Library of Congress Cataloging in Publication data available.

ISBN 1 902618 88 2

Contents

Before you start squishing...

Long before we humans first appeared on this little planet of ours, bugs scuttled, crawled, creeped, hovered and buzzed about.

Insects have been around for millions of years, and yet bugs still remain a huge mystery to us. Around a million different insects have been categorized, but some scientists believe that up to 30 million are yet to be discovered. Beetles, for instance, make up nearly a third of all creatures in the animal kingdom. Add spiders, scorpions, and microscopic bugs to the list, and you're talking about an awful lot of critters!

Not all bugs are the sort that have you reaching for the insecticide, though. Some bugs exist only as products of an active imagination – the sort of incredible insects that science fiction throws up at us to invade our nightmares! But there are other bugs that we should fear even more – dreaded viruses that can strike us down when we least expect it. You'll find the full lowdown on all these bugs in this book too.

One final thought for anyone who runs screaming from the bathroom every time a spider shows up. If you're the sort who stomps on bugs, you'd better watch out. This is their world too – a bug's world, as it happens – and these guys have been around long before we turned up on the scene. Squish today, and it may well be you who's getting squished tomorrow...

Bad bugs

These are the ones you love to hate, the bugs that strike terror into every heart. They're living proof that not all bugs are humankind's little helpers. These guys are mean, keen killing machines. Don't say you were never warned...

BLACK WIDOW

What is it? A deadly
web-spinning spider.
Lives: North, Central and
South America, southern
Europe, Africa, Asia, Australia
and New Zealand. Likes to hide out in its web in barns,
sheds and other buildings.
Appearance: The deadly female black widow has a black
shiny body roughly the size of a pea. It grows to about
1.5in long with its legs extended. A red or yellow mark in
an hourglass shape can be found on its belly.
Weapons: Its fangs can deliver a venomous bite that is said
to be 15 times more lethal than that of a rattlesnake. Ouch.
Case file: If bitten the symptoms include excruciating pain,
continuous sweating and dribbling, hallucinations, spasms,
and then the victim eventually stops breathing. Not very
pleasant. The black widow frequently hides in clothes and

shoes. It's even been known to spin webs across toilet seats. Could be nasty.

Strange but true: The black widow is so named after the female's unfortunate tendency to eat her male partner after mating. So much for table manners!

Fear factor: 🕷️🕷️🕷️🕷️🕷️🕷️🕷️🕷️

As well as being an expert in deadly bites, this eight-legged monster likes hiding in your clothes and bed. Be afraid, be very afraid.

Bug Laugh!

How do spiders communicate?
On the World Wide Web!

COCKROACH

What is it? Germ-carrying household pest.

Lives: In your house, although you may not see these light-sensitive beasts as they like to hide in the dark.

Appearance: Horrible. It has a flat oval body with long legs that help it to scuttle fast. Also has claws that it uses to climb your walls.

Case file: Cockroaches love hiding out in houses. All they need is water and the temperature to be over 18 degrees centigrade. As a scavenger, the cockroach will eat anything. Yes, that includes dead animals, paper, and unwanted food. It breeds quickly as well – the female will lay more than 30 eggs every 25 days!

Don't panic! Just keep your house clean and dry, fix any leaky taps, and don't leave any food or dirty dishes out and you should be able to avoid a cockroach invasion.

Fear factor: 🪳🪳🪳🪳🪳

The germs may be the real danger, but who likes roaches?

Bug Bite

 A cockroach has its skeleton on the outside of its body. That means you can step on these beasts and they're still able to scuttle away!

 These guys have serious staying power! Cockroaches have lived on earth for about 250 million years.

FAT-TAILED SCORPION

What is it? The world's deadliest scorpion.

Lives: You'll find them in the driest areas of North Africa and the Sahara Desert.

Weapons: Its poisonous sting. The fat-tailed scorpion has a venomous sting the equivalent of a cobra bite. Once struck, the venom can kill a man in seven hours, or a dog in just seven minutes!

Case file: This scorpion, like many of its kind, is better adapted to hot temperatures and dry conditions than any other living creature. The secret to this is its wax covering that helps the fat-tailed scorpion stay nice and moist in arid conditions.

Fear factor:

If you see this scorpion, just run. One sting means curtains.

Bug Bite

A scorpion is capable of losing as much as 40 percent of its body fluid and still living to see another day. Phew!

FUNNEL WEB SPIDER

What is it? A deadly venomous spider.

Lives: The funnel web is only found in Australia, particularly in the south-east area, and Tasmania. It hangs out in burrows but also in trees.

Appearance: Brown or black, measuring up to 2in long.

Weapons: Its fangs which produce venom.

Case file: The Sydney funnel web spider is particularly aggressive when disturbed and will rear up into a strike position. Funnel webs have been known to burrow into house foundations and the male often enters homes, especially after a sudden downpour in the summer months. It has amazing fangs that can penetrate even a child's fingernail. If bitten, it can be fatal. A bite will throw you into shock; your muscles will twitch, you sweat, cry and dribble. They can also cause brain damage.

Don't panic! Thankfully an anti-venom was invented in 1980. If you get to a hospital in time, you should be OK.

Fear factor:

This spider has a venom that is particularly dangerous to humans, and a habit of not being afraid to use it.

Bug Bite

The funnel web is named after the woven funnel-shaped entrance to its burrow.

GIANT MAGGOT

What is it? A massive mutated maggot made famous in cult sci-fi TV series Doctor Who.

Lives: In the Welsh village of Llanfairfach.

Appearance: Like maggots but much, MUCH bigger. Oh, and it has a mysterious green glow.

Grub: Green radioactive slime.

Weapons: The giant maggot can kill a human with its venomous bite which turns its victim bright green during a slow, painful death. One victim was a Welsh miner who met up with the maggot down a mine shaft.

Case file: The giant maggot was created by chemical waste pumped from a Global Chemicals plant. The director of the plant had been taken over by a computer called BOSS (Bimorphic Organisational Systems Supervisor) and it had a master plan to hijack all the world's computers. The Time Lord Doctor Who discovered this plot and broke BOSS's control of the plant director who then set the chemical plant to self-destruct.

Don't panic! The giant maggots were destroyed with a type of fungus just as they were on the verge of transforming themselves into giant insects.

Fear factor: 🐜🐜🐜🐜🐜

The giant maggot sent a shiver down the spine of many youngsters at the time, but stay away from radioactive slime and the danger should be minimal.

MILLENNIUM BUG

What is it? A glitch in computer chips that will strike come 31 December 1999 – with disastrous effects.

Lives: Computers, hospital equipment, cash point machines, toasters, power stations, jumbo jets… anywhere you can find a computer chip, which is pretty much everywhere nowadays. It is estimated there are 200 billion micro-chips in the world today.

Appearance: Unknown, but it's lurking in your video player somewhere, you can be sure.

Weapons: The ability to make computers fail or make them think it's 1 January 1900 (before they were invented). This is sure to send them (and of course, us) crazy.

Case file: The Millennium Bug all came about because

computers were designed to recognize dates in two digits instead of four digits (or 99 instead of 1999). So come the year 2000, many will reset themselves to 00. It's all being blamed on computer programmers who never imagined that many of these chips would still be around for the next millennium. Whoops!

Panic! Some people are predicting that planes will crash, banks will wipe out people's savings, life support machines in hospitals will fail and more importantly, TVs won't work. Serious stuff.

Don't panic! Thankfully both governments and computer chip manufacturers realized the problem and have been bug-busting ever since. Some experts reckon it's all too little, too late. All computer chips made today should be Millennium Bug (or Year 2000) proof.

Fear factor: 🐜🐜🐜🐜🐜🐜🐜🐜
Pretty scary stuff, although no one is 100 percent sure what will happen. It might be wise to lock yourself away with a supply of chocolate and comics come 31 December 1999, just in case.

MOSQUITO

What is it? The most dangerous insect on Earth. It loves humans, especially sucking our blood, and infecting us with some of the world's most disgusting diseases.

Appearance: These flying insects are only about a quarter of an inch long. Small then, but definitely deadly.

Lives: A cosmopolitan character, the mossie lives all around the world including the Arctic. But the deadly germ carrying variety lives in hot, moist lands near the equator. They're found all over Africa.

Grub: This predator loves nothing more than sucking the blood from frogs, snakes, birds, cows, horses and – here's the scary bit – people.

Weapons: Its six needle-like parts called stylets stab through the victim's skin. Only the female mosquito bites as she needs blood to feed the eggs which grow inside her body. Even the mosquitoes that don't carry life-threatening diseases can deliver a nasty bite that is painful and extremely itchy.

Case file: The mosquito spreads malaria that infects at least 200 million people worldwide a year. It kills one million youngsters in Africa alone. What's more, it also passes on the germs that cause elephantiasis and yellow fever. Most males live only seven to ten days, yet the deadly female can survive more than 30 days.

Strange but true: Some mosquitoes can gulp down one and a half times their body weight in one blood drinking session alone!

Fear factor: ⚶⚶⚶⚶⚶⚶⚶⚶
Small it may be, but this blood sucker is the deadliest creature known to man. Only protection known is vaccination jabs to prevent disease, nets to keep the

blood-sucking pests at bay, and chemical insecticides to keep their numbers down. Never underestimate the mosquito. It is a killer.

PALESTINE YELLOW

What is it? A deadly scorpion. Also known as the African gold scorpion.

Lives: North Africa and the Middle East.

Weapons: A narrow tail that has a pair of poisonous glands and a sting at the end.

Case file: Although this scorpion mainly uses its venomous sting in self defence, it does sting humans it considers dangerous when it is scared. The amount of venom it injects is fortunately very small, and has little effect on adults. But for children under five, it can prove nasty. Symptoms include: intense pain, tightening of the throat, slurred speech, sweating, vomiting and a blueing of the lips… then death. Not nice at all!

Fear factor: 🦂🦂🦂🦂🦂🦂
Normally quite docile in the burning sun but, if disturbed, it will have no hesitation in using its deadly sting.

SLUG

What is it? The gardener's number one enemy.

Lives: In your garden and vegetable patch, ruining all your parents' hard work.

Appearance: A snail without the house on its back. Also has a pair of feelers with eyes on them.

Case file: The slug is considered a garden pest

as it has a huge appetite for plants, leaving big holes in leaves and destroying fruit and vegetables (tomatoes, strawberries, cabbage and lettuces). Gardeners get rid of their slug invaders by setting traps and using poisonous pellets. Some even use beer traps to entice slugs. They're attracted by the yeast, before they drown in the stuff.

Fear factor:

Give these guys a break. OK, it's ugly and no one seems to care for it much, but is it really that bad a bug? At least it eats its greens.

Bug Laugh!

What do you call a homeless snail? A slug!

SUPERBUG

What is it? Medical science's biggest challenge – and threat – for the next millennium.

Lives: Superbugs thrive in the human body and eventually kill an infected person. Scientists have captured them under the microscope, in a desperate bid to find a way to beat these killers.

Appearance: Tiny, bad bacteria, but with the kind of super-tough resistance that makes cockroaches sound puny.

Case file: In the first half of the 20th century, medicine made great strides against harmful bacterial diseases with the development of antibiotics. Yet some of these bacteria have evolved and have now become resistant to these treatments. Doctors believe this may have happened because the bugs have got wise to the drugs, and become immune to them. These life-threatening superbugs are bound to stage a comeback in the 21st century. Already certain strains of the deadly diseases pneumonia, tuberculosis, and typhoid have developed resistance to certain antibiotics. Seriously scary stuff.

Fear factor: 🐜🐜🐜🐜🐜🐜🐜🐜

There are worrying signs in poor Third World countries that superbugs are definitely on the increase. Scientists and governments will have to work around the clock to tighten up on procedures and make sure these superbugs are met head on with all drugs blazing.

VENOM

Who is he? Spider-Man's deadly rival.

Lives: Unknown, but reports suggest he may be camped out underground in San Francisco.

Appearance: Muscle-bound baddie in an all-black body stocking with a white spider on his chest.

Weapons: Super-strength, bullet-resistant suit, and the ability to change shape and camouflage himself.

Case file: Venom started his evil beginnings as a living costume before finding a host – reporter Eddie Brock –

a man with a grudge against Spider-Man. He is the evil opposite of Spider-Man, Peter Parker. Venom gradually grew into something of a hero, and Brock's one time cell mate, serial killer Cletus Kasady, became infected by the Venom costume and turned into Carnage – wreaking havoc on a far greater scale than Venom ever did.

Don't panic! Later, Spider-Man and Venom were seen reluctantly joining forces to combat Carnage.

Fear Factor: 🕷 🕷 🕷 🕷

Though he's something of a reformed character now, he can still be a bit of a bad bug.

Bug Laugh!

**Did you hear about the spider who went into shock?
He found a big hairy man in the bath!**

Bodacious bugs

Some bugs are so cleverly
adapted that you just can't help
but marvel at them. This chapter is
dedicated to all those amazing breeds of
bug. All these bugs are awesome in their own
different way. Don't try and understand them –
just believe...

ADAM ANT

Who is he? Punk leader of cult pop group The Ants in the early 1980s.

Lives: London, England, although his precise location since he left the Ants is unknown.

Appearance: Shocking. Adam Ant was part of the "New Romantic" era, and famous for wearing frilly shirts, pirate costumes and Native American Indian make-up. Easily recognized by the white lines painted across his face.

Abilities: He was able to sing at high pitch and dance in a strange kind of tribal style.

Case file: After a string of hit songs such as Antmusic, Stand and Deliver, and Prince Charming, Antmania gripped Britain. Yet just as quickly as it arrived, Antmania had disappeared by 1982. By 1985 Adam Ant had, er, ants in his pants and swapped his costumes and make-up for more costumes and make-up of a different kind – he became an actor.

Wow factor: 🐜🐜🐜🐜🐜

Word of warning: if you fancy recreating the look at home, ask permission first. Mum may take exception to you diving into her make-up bag!

Bug Laugh!

How do you know if an ant has been flying in your house?
Check your ant-i-aircraft radar!

ARMY ANT

What is it? Ferocious hunter that travels in huge colonies.

Lives: Can be seen marching in columns across North and South America, and Africa. Unlike other ant species, they do not have a permanent nest.

Appearance: Usually seen in their millions. The colony is divided into different types: the queen, the males and the workers. Larger worker ants are called soldiers.

Grub: Any insect or spider that is unfortunate enough to come in the way of an army ant colony will not live long. Even large animals such as snakes have been known to fall prey to this military muncher.

Weapons: Its sheer weight in numbers, its long biting jaws (called mandibles) and its fearlessness. Some soldier ants also carry a sting.

Case file: Most army ant colonies have from 10,000 to several million members. When resting, the colony will cluster together in a large bunch on a tree or in a hollow trunk. Some army ant colonies will spend weeks hunting before resting to allow the queen to lay her eggs.

Wow factor: 🐜🐜🐜🐜🐜

We humans are pretty safe from these super predators, but you have to admire their organization!

Bug Laugh!
What do you call an ant covered in glue?
A stick insect!

Scientists believe ants developed from wasps more than 100 million years ago.

 The legionary ant and the driver ant are also species of the army ant.

ASSASSIN BUG

What is it? Ruthless bug carnivore.

Lives: All over the world.

Appearance: The most striking thing about an assassin bug is its powerful curved beak – a tool of ruthless efficiency.

Grub: Ants, cockroaches, even birds and small reptiles have felt the assassin's attack.

Weapons: Apart from its deadly beak, this bug is equipped with powerful forelegs that can seize its prey. These legs have sticky pads made up of thousands of tiny hairs that can cling to their victims to stop them from getting away.

Case file: The assassin bug feeds by pushing its beak into its prey and injecting a toxic liquid. This poison liquifies the nerves and tissue of its prey, and the assassin bug sucks out the mushy inside – one super slurpy shake coming up! The deadly saliva of the assassin bug can kill a cockroach in only four seconds. As for a caterpillar 400 times its weight, the assassin can polish one of those off in just 10 seconds.

Wow factor:

For its size, it is probably the most effective and ruthless killer on the planet. Thankfully for us, its size means we don't have to worry too much about these bad guys.

Bug Bite

Assassin bugs get their name from the speed at which they can grab and poison their victims.

CENTIPEDE

What is it? A land-loving cousin of crabs and shrimps, or a "100-legged" worm, as its name suggests.

Lives: Anywhere hot and steamy.

Appearance: A caterpillar with legs, legs and more legs. A centipede can come in a rainbow of colors, from light yellow to dark or reddish brown. They can be anything from 1in to a whopping 12in long.

Grub: Worms, snails and other insects.

Weapons: A centipede has a set of powerful jaws that traps its prey before its fangs deliver a deadly poison. The fangs also come in handy if there's a fight.

Case file: A centipede's poison can cause harm to humans, but in most cases it's no more dangerous than your average bee sting.

Strange but true: Should you wish to count a centipede's sets of legs, you'd be amazed to find that the number is always odd. Now that is odd…

Wow factor:

All those legs, and how come they don't fall over?

Bug Bite

There are some 2,800 types of centipede. The largest, the giant desert centipede, kills and eats small lizards!

FIREFLY

What is it? The bug that likes to be seen at night.

Lives: Usually spotted flying around somewhere damp and dull, like a meadow.

Appearance: Glowing. The firefly is actually a type of beetle. That means it has two sets of wings, one of which it uses to fly.

Grub: As larvae, the firefly will eat snails and earthworms, but once an adult in full glow, it will not eat anything except nectar from flowers. Fussy, isn't it?

Case file: The firefly's glow comes from a chemical reaction in the bug's abdomen. The light is "cold light" as it produces no heat – a lot like the glow-in-the-dark sticks you get for parties. The firefly uses this flashing light to attract a mate. The male will fly around showing off until a female who likes the look of him flashes a signal back.

Wow factor: 🐜🐜🐜🐜🐜🐜
The firefly just comes and glows as it pleases!

Bug Bite

 Fireflies are also known as lightning bugs in some parts of the world.

 Each firefly species has its own individual light pattern. Talk about flashy...

GRASSHOPPER

What is it? The greatest long jumper in the bug kingdom.

Lives: The hopper is seen in meadows and fields all over the world.

Appearance: Very close resemblance to both the locust and katydid. In fact, they are all part of the same family.

Case file: The grasshopper can jump 20 times the length of its body. That means if it was the size of a human, the grasshopper would jump about 40 yards – that's over four times the length of the long jump world record! It gets this amazing ability from powerful muscles in its hind legs. The grasshopper needs it though, as it's the favorite snack of beetles, birds, mice, snakes and spiders. As well as its jump, the grasshopper will fly away or blend into its surroundings to avoid predators. Clever at camouflage, grasshoppers found among leaves will be green-colored while those found on the ground will be brown.

Wow factor: 🐜🐜🐜🐜🐜🐜
The hopper is the lord of the leap, sending any hungry predators hopping mad with one wondrous thrust of its legs.

Bug Laugh!

What do you call a bug on a pogo stick?
A grasshopper!

HONEY BEE

What is it? A buzzing, flying marvel.

Lives: Honey bees live in hives. These double as their storage space, and are usually a hollow tree or a box that contains the honeycomb. The honeycomb is used to store food and raise their young.

Appearance: Striped yellow and black with four wings. You'll have seen them buzzing around the flowers in your garden or at the local park.

Grub: Flowers provide bees with the nectar they use to make honey. It tastes pretty good too, as we humans know – we like a dollop of honey on our toast!

Weapons: The honey bee has a sting which pumps a poison into the victim. The sting detaches after the bee has used it, and the bee will die soon afterwards. As you'd imagine, a honey bee will only use its sting in a case of an extreme emergency.

Case file: Honey bees, like other bees and ants, are called social insects as they live together in huge colonies. A colony will consist of one queen, tens of thousands of workers, and a few hundred drones. Worker bees spend their time in search of nectar which they swallow to take back to the hive. Then they spit the nectar up to be stored, and when it dries it turns into honey.

Don't panic! Only female honey bees sting. She will only use her sting if she feels that she or her hive is under threat. After all, while that sting may hurt you, remember it's going to kill the bee!

Wow factor:

The honey bee is an amazing candy factory with wings.

Bug Bite

The buzzing of a bee is the sound of its wings vibrating. Bees are expert fliers and can both hover and fly.

Bug Laugh!

Patient: Doctor! Doctor! I think I'm turning into a bee!

Doctor: Oh buzz off, will you, I've got a room full of patients!

LADYBUG

What is it? The princess of the bug world.

Lives: Flying around plants and crops, showing off.

Appearance: Rather flash. Bright red or yellow with some fetching white, red or black spots. Very distinctive.

Grub: Despite its delicate appearance, the ladybug loves to tuck in to an insect. You'd think they'd see it coming, wouldn't you?

Case file: The ladybug is actually a beetle. Farmers and gardeners love them as they snack on pests, such as aphids, that ruin their plants and crops.

Wow factor: 🐜🐜🐜🐜🐜🐜🐜🐜

Very trendy, the ladybug looks good and it knows it.

MILLIPEDE

What is it? A centipede with even more legs.

Lives: Dark, damp places – under a nice stone or a cosy rotting log is ideal.

Appearance: This walking worm is hard to find as it's quite shy, but it's generally brown or black in color, much like its surroundings.

Grub: Bit of a scavenger, the millipede will eat decaying plants and rotten leaves. Occasionally treats itself to a fresh stem or the odd root.

Case file: Similar to the centipede but this leggy legend has two pairs of feet for each body segment, as opposed to the centipede's one pair per segment. Despite the name meaning "1,000 legged" no millipede actually has a thousand legs (apparently someone has counted them). Some millipedes have a total of 115 pairs of limbs.

A millipede can whiff a bit as it gives off a bad odor. It also produces an irritating liquid than can cause allergic reactions, so you'd be best advised not to touch them with your bare hands.

Strange but true: Certain species of millipede produce deadly cyanide poison on their bodies!

Wow factor:

More legs than a centipede (who's counting?) but neither as outgoing, nor as colorful.

Bug Laugh!

Did you hear about the centipedes vs millipedes football match?

By the time the teams had their boots on, the ref had blown the final whistle!

MONARCH BUTTERFLY

What is it? Long-distance king of the butterfly world.

Lives: The migrating monarch can be seen in Canada and the northern United States in the summer, and Florida, California and Mexico in the winter months.

Appearance: Thousands of black and orange colored monarchs can be spotted heading north or south, depending on the time of year.

Case file: This remarkable butterfly's migration is an annual journey of more than 2,000 miles. As you'd expect, it's not without its perils. The monarch faces mountains, strong winds and predators. Once it arrives in Florida, California or Mexico, it spends the winter resting and conserving energy for the return flight. Because of its lifespan, an adult monarch will probably not live long enough to make the return journey. Shame, huh?

Wow factor: 🐜🐜🐜🐜🐜🐜🐜🐜🐜
The monarch is a long-distance champ.

Bug Bite

The sight of thousands of monarchs covering trees is a big tourist attraction. One Californian town called Pacific Grove is nicknamed "Butterfly Town, USA" for the huge number of monarchs that gather there.

Bug Laugh!
Did you hear the joke about the butterfly? I'll only tell you if you promise not to spread it!

Bug Laugh!
Why did the butterfly go into the betting shop? Because he fancied a little flutter!

SPITTING SPIDER

What is it? A small arachnid.

Lives: In wooden areas, under trees or leaves.

Appearance: Quite a small spider (about a quarter of an inch long), it is pale yellow to dark brown in color.

Grub: Small insects.

Case file: What makes this spider pretty special is its clever way of catching prey – by spitting a poisonous silk at it! The spitting spider is quite a careful hunter and mainly sneaks around for food at night. Once it has spotted a sleeping insect, it measures up the distance before squeezing the back of its body and sending a venomous strand of silk shooting out at its prey. The victim can't move. Dinner is served!

Wow factor: 🐜🐜🐜🐜🐜🐜🐜

This spider may be quite small and slow, but with that clever little spitting trick up its sleeve, who needs to go running around in search of snacks?

38

TRAP-DOOR SPIDER

What is it? A cunning arachnid.

Lives: Holed up in a cleverly disguised burrow, usually in a warm climate.

Appearance: You won't find a photo of this guy anywhere! This very timid spider rarely leaves its lair.

Grub: Unsuspecting insects.

Weapons: Speed, cunning, and two poisonous fangs.

Case file: The trap-door spider digs a burrow and covers the entrance with a lid or trap made of silk and mud. The spider waits behind the trap door until its unsuspecting insect prey walks by. Quick as a flash, the spider jumps out, grabs the victim and poisons it before disappearing back down the trap with its ready meal.

Wow rating:

The trap-door spider is a brainy little bug – much too cunning for its insect dinners!

Bug Laugh!

Diner: Waiter! Waiter! There's a spider in my soup!

Waiter: That's all right, sir. It'll be after the fly...

Bug Bite

You don't have to worry about the trap-door spider invading your nightmares. The shy critter rarely leaves its burrow and raises its young deep underground. But boy, can this guy burrow – some of its tunnels are more than 10in deep and over 1in wide!

Tiny bugs

Some bugs are so small,
you could almost be forgiven for
overlooking them. But this collection of
microscopic marvels simply can't be ignored.
Whether you're suffering from a sore throat or
your hairy hound is having a good scratch, you
can't escape the reminders
that tiny bugs
also share our
world. Just be
grateful that
these titchy
critters don't
grow up into
anything
bigger…

ANT-MAN

Who is he? A super hero and founding member of the Avengers. Also known as the scientist Henry Pym.

Lives: At a top secret (so secret it can't be revealed) location in the United States of America.

Appearance: Ant-sized with a red and blue body suit and helmet. Often appears on the back of a flying ant.

Weapons: Ant-Man has a cybernetic helmet that enables him to communicate with an army of ants.

Case file: Scientist Henry Pym discovered the ability to shrink to the size of an ant in 1962 before reinventing himself as Ant-Man. Ant-Man fought foreign spies, the criminal scientist Egghead, as well as Scarlet Beetle, the evil mutated bug out to conquer the world. Partnered with fellow super hero Wasp, Henry Pym hit hard times in the 1980s after exposure to strange chemical fumes. He became mentally unstable and was court-martialed by the Avengers. The final straw came when arch-enemy Egghead framed Ant-Man and he was imprisoned. Today Henry Pym still serves in the Avengers as Giant-Man.

Fear factor:

Never the most dynamic of the Avengers. Still, when no other super hero is available, you wouldn't say no – even if he is hard to spot.

Bug Laugh!
What do you call someone who sells very old insects?
An ant-ique dealer!

APHID

What is it? Plant-sucking bug.

Appearance: Small, the aphid has a beak that it uses to suck up plant juices.

Grub: Plants and lots of them.

Case file: This bug can be a plant pest if it's not controlled. Thankfully, nature has its own answer to pest control with ladybugs, birds, wasps, and other bugs who just love to tuck into an aphid feast!

Strange but true! Aphids are an ant's best friend as the aphid secretes sugary "honeydew" which the ants love to eat. Ants even babysit them – they keep them in their nests during winter and shelter aphids from the rain!

Fear factor:
Harmless in small numbers, large groups can cause flower lovers to reach for the spray guns.

DOG FLEA

What is it? Your pet's worst enemy.

Lives: On your mutt, jumping around deep inside its coat.

Appearance: This microscopic, wingless parasite has a flattened body to allow it to crawl between hairs in your dog's fur. Dog fleas are usually pale to dark-reddish brown, depending upon whether or not they've had a bite to eat.

Grub: Dog blood – and failing that, they'll go for your cat.

Weapons: Piercing mouths that puncture your dog's skin to form a channel to suck blood.

Case file: These fleas have claws at the tips
of their legs that enable them to cling on
to a dog's fur no matter how much our
four-legged friend scratches, shakes or
bites. Dogs are often left with an uncomfortable red
itchy bump thanks to their fleas' feasting.
If food is scarce, a dog flea can wait one or
two months without eating, waiting for its
next doggie dinner.

Fear factor:

Harmless to us but very irritating when you see poor Rover
scratching continuously. Often leaves pet owners feeling
very itchy for no reason at all.

Bug Bite

With its six long legs, the dog flea can long
jump more than 12in.

Bug Laugh!

**Why don't fleas take
the train?
They prefer to
'itchhike!**

Bug Laugh!

**Why did the flea
get the sack?
It wasn't up
to scratch!**

DUNG BEETLE

What is it? A scavenging beetle.

Lives: Inside animal dung. Some even make a ball of dung, roll it around until they find a nice spot, and bury it.

Grub: Not only does it live in animal dung, it loves eating it as well and will eat its own weight in dung every day.

Case file: Although it sounds pretty disgusting, the dung beetle actually performs an essential role as it helps to clean the environment. It also helps enrich the soil by burying the dung in the ground, putting vital nutrients back where they're needed.

Fear factor: 🐛🐛

They may be nature's little helpers, but they do leave a nasty niff about the place.

Bug Laugh!

Why did the beetle run across the top of the cornflake box?

Because it said "tear along the dotted line!"

EARWIG

What is it? The bug with the pincers at the back.

Lives: Anywhere that's nice and moist, such as under stones, or in rotting tree bark.

Appearance: An earwig has a hard, shiny armor with long feelers, but it's best recognized by its large pair of pincers on its rear.

Grub: It's carnivorous and tucks into caterpillars and snails.

Case file: Ever wondered how earwigs got their name? In days of yore, it was believed that earwigs crawled in to people's ears while they slept. They don't.

Fear factor:

The look may be mean, but those pincers are all show.

Bug Laugh!

What did one earwig say to the other as they jumped off a cliff? Earwig-gooooooooooh!

Bug Bite

Although earwigs may destroy fruit and flowers, they also help farmers by eating thrips, snails and caterpillars.

HONEY ANT

What is it? The ant with the sweet tooth.

Lives: In huge nests in dry, warm regions of the world.

Grub: Honeydew – a sweet substance secreted by other insects and plants.

Case file: Also known as the honey-pot ant, the honey ant gathers honeydew to feed to special worker ants called repletes. These repletes serve as living larders and become so swollen with honeydew that they cannot walk and just hang from a ceiling in the nest. When it gets a little peckish, the honey ant just taps the replete with its antennae, and the replete regurgitates some honeydew for the ant to eat. Hmm, how appetizing…

Fear factor: But would you eat candy that's already been in somebody else's stomach?

MAYFLY

What is it? Short-lived flyer.

Lives: Found in and around ponds or streams usually in spring time … but only for a few hours. It's got the shortest adult life of any insect.

Appearance: It has four lacy wings (so it's not really a true fly as they only have two wings) and a slender forked tail.

Grub: Eat? This bug has no time for food!

Case file: A young mayfly spends anything between a few months and a year as a "nymph," swimming around in a pond, before transforming into an adult mayfly. During its brief adult life, a mayfly must mate and lay eggs back in the water … very quickly! It plays a vital role in the food chain: a swarm of hatching mayflies, numbering millions, provides vital food for fish. A large gang of mayflies means it's a clean stream, but if no mayflies are around it's usually a sure sign that the water supply is dirty.

Fear factor:

Frightening?! You should feel sorry for this short-lived bug. So much to do, so little time to do it in …

Bug Bite

One type of female mayfly lives for only five minutes! Wonder how she manages to squeeze everything in?!

SILVERFISH

What is it? Wingless household pest that pops up when you least expect.

Lives: Prefers its living space to be cold, damp and moist.

Appearance: Silver in color with two long antennae and a segmented body. It's a pretty nifty mover too!

Grub: This pest loves tucking into starchy items like your clothes, wallpaper and books.

Fear factor: ⸝⸜ ⸝⸜ ⸝⸜ ⸝⸜
Well, they can give you a bit of a start if you find one in the middle of a horror story …

SLAVE MAKER

What is it? The ant that likes to command and conquer. It's the Alexander the Great of the ant species, and it's out to rule the world.

Lives: In the nests of other ants that it has taken over by force. The slave maker can be discovered in the cooler regions of North America, Europe and Asia.

Appearance: Highly organized, social insect.

Case file: Slave makers raid the nests of other ants and carry off the pupae (eggs). When the pupae become adults, they help with the work in the slave makers' colony and end up as their "slaves."

Fear factor: ⸝⸜ ⸝⸜ ⸝⸜ ⸝⸜
Nice work – if you can get it!

49

Bug Bite

 An ant's jaws, or mandibles, move from side to side rather than up and down.

 Some tropical ants have underground nests that stretch 12 yards below ground!

STREPTOCOCCUS

What is it? Harmful, microscopic bugs.

Lives: They thrive in the warmth inside your body, waiting to breed and cause damage to your health.

Appearance: Streptococcus is a bacterial bug commonly found in the throat and on the skin. Most of the time, they pose little threat to us.

Case file: These bad bacteria are responsible for giving us sore throats, earache and skin infections. They can produce poisonous substances in your body called toxins which make you ill. In more serious (but much less common) streptococcal infections, scarlet fever and tonsillitis can strike you down.

Don't panic! Your doctor can prescribe antibiotic medicine (such as penicillin) that can destroy steptococcus bacteria when you're poorly.

Fear factor: 🐜🐜🐜🐜🐜🐜

Sore throats aren't nice but docs have 'em under control.

Bug Laugh!
What do bugs do if they get a sore throat?
Gargle with ant-iseptic!

Bug Bite

There are hundreds of different types of bacteria. Another bad bacteria is staphylococcus which causes boils and infects wounds.

TERMITE

What is it? Wood-chomping pest that hangs out in huge, hungry gangs.

Lives: Underground or in your walls. The tropical termite lives in huge nests that are more than 6 yards high.

Appearance: Six-legged, although what it looks like depends on whether it is a reproductive, worker or soldier termite. However, they all have a nice set of gnashers.

Grub: Floorboards, paper, furniture … in fact, anything wooden that they can get their teeth into. Microscopic bugs inside the termite actually break down the wood they munch so that they can digest it.

Case file: A termite will often live in a colony with over 100

million other termites. There are three classes of termite. The reproductive termite (king or queen) produces eggs and can grow to 20,000 times the size of a worker termite, especially as it lays about 30,000 eggs a day. The worker builds the colony, looks after the eggs and basically panders to the other termites. The soldier termite is in charge of security and has to defend the colony.

Strange but true: Boy, do these guys get hungry. They can reduce a whole house to termite waste and sawdust in less than three years.

Fear factor:

Just don't let them near your mother's best dining room table or there will be trouble!

Bug Laugh!

Did you hear about the termite who got tummy ache?
It was a bad case of wood poisoning!

Bug Bite

Termites are very fussy about keeping their colony clean and will even eat their dead mates to keep the place spick and span. Saves on vacuuming, I guess …

TICK

What is it? The slightly larger relation of the mite.

Lives: It's a parasite, which means it relies on other animals to provide it with food and housing. In this case chickens, dogs, pigs, horses, sheep and, unfortunately, humans.

Appearance: A tick has eight legs that stick out like a crab's, and a beak that it uses to drain blood from its host.

Weapons: The tick is a disease carrier and transfers these infections to the blood of whatever it is feeding on.

Case file: An attack by a tick can lead to a person being paralyzed until it is removed. The deer tick, through its bacteria-laden saliva, transmits Lyme disease to humans.

Don't panic! We need to protect against the tick, especially in woody or bushy areas in the summer. That means wearing long-sleeved shirts with your pants tucked in to socks. Oh, and a big can of insect repellent may be a good idea too.

Fear factor:

It's not a pleasant bug to be seen with, but think yourself lucky – it's more of a problem for cattle and sheep than it is for us humans.

Bug Bite

Mites and ticks are relatives of spiders and scorpions – they are not insects.

WEEVIL

What is it? A beetle with a big nose.

Lives: Wherever there is the chance to feast on plants, fruit or crops. And yes, that could mean your garden!

Appearance: Small, about half an inch long, and usually grayish-brown to black.

Grub: Anything vegetarian – wheat, apple, flowers, plums. Weevils are not particularly fussy eaters.

Weapons: Its ugly snout and enormous appetite.

Case file: Weevils are the farmers' and gardeners' worst nightmare, hence its nickname "the Jaws of the garden." Both grubs (baby) and adult weevils cause damage to all kinds of crops and plants. Weevils lay their eggs in the stalk, seed or fruit of a plant and once they're hatched the grubs feast themselves silly. The US Department of Agriculture takes the weevil so seriously they've imported thousands of weevil-eating insects to battle this plant pest. Fruit weevils like fruit, the rice weevil likes rice, the grain weevil likes, er, grain … I guess you get the picture, right?

Fear factor: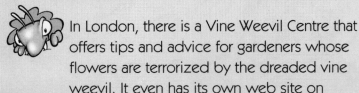

The mere mention of the W word will send most gardeners into either a cold sweat or a ferocious rage. These bugs are some crazy wrecking-crew and professional plant growers' nightmares are plagued by these little demons.

Bug Bite

In London, there is a Vine Weevil Centre that offers tips and advice for gardeners whose flowers are terrorized by the dreaded vine weevil. It even has its own web site on www.vine.weevil.org.uk

Body bugs

OK, here's the bad news. Your body is one great big bug fest! They're inside it, on the surface of your skin, and you may even have a couple of visitors on your head (feeling itchy are we?). And while some of these may be unwelcome, others are essential to your health and well-being. The good news is, we're not talking big bugs here. In fact, some are so tiny, you're not going to be able to see them – unless you have a powerful microscope to hand!

BED BUG

What is it? Blood sucking parasite that comes out at night.

Lives: In your bed, laundry, pillow and sheets.

Appearance: They are quite elusive fellows. An unfed bed bug is pale and small, but after a midnight blood snack it transforms into a dark red color and swells in size.

Grub: Blood. While you sleep peacefully a bed bug will sneak up and feed on you. After it has sucked itself to bursting point, usually in about three minutes, an itchy, red blotch will appear to say it's called in for a bite to eat.

Case file: A bed bug may be hard to spot, but you'll be able to smell them all right! They give off an oily liquid that stinks. It only takes a couple of days before a bed bug will be looking for another meal of blood. If they do fancy feasting on your flesh, you'd best call in the professionals – insecticide is the only way to rid your bed of the bug.

Gross factor: 🐛🐛🐛🐛🐛🐛🐛

The vampire of the bug world. Thank heavens they aren't any bigger than they are.

Bug Bite

The bed bug has been sucking our blood since we were living in caves millions of years ago.

DUST MITE

What is it? A dust mite is a microscopic relative of spiders and scorpions.

Lives: These mites love to make their home in your house. You'll find them hanging out in a particularly snug carpet, a bed, a pillow ... well, anywhere really.

Appearance: Oval shaped with little paddles to help them

move around. Dust mites are also very tiny – you could get almost a dozen of them on this full stop.

Grub: These mini monsters tuck in to flakes of human skin. They also like munching on old hair and fingernails.

Strange but true: They are impossible to destroy. Even if you vacuumed a small carpet for 20 minutes, you would only remove about 2 percent of the millions of mites that lurk within it! Dust mites cause some people to sneeze, wheeze and scratch.

Gross factor: 🐛 🐛 🐛 🐛
Tough they may be, but the tiny dust mite is quite happy tucking into the skin your body dumps all around the house.

FLU BUG

What is it? A virus that makes you feel very ill.

Lives: In you – giving you a sore throat, aching arms and legs, a headache, and a fever. Not very nice at all.

Appearance: As a virus, the flu bug is a microscopic creature and is easily passed on through the air when you breath or sneeze.

Case file: Doctors have identified three types of flu bug (or influenza) – A, B and C. Those particularly vulnerable to the flu bug are the ill and elderly – their immune systems are not always strong enough to fight off an attack. A vaccine is available but it has to be prepared in advance every year to be effective against the next strain of flu bug.

Just as your body builds up an immunity to one type (or strain) of flu bug, along comes another. This is because the flu virus is very clever and can mutate itself to trick your immune system.

Don't panic! If you've got the flu, there's not much you can do but clamber into bed for 48 hours and drink plenty of water. Rest is vital to a full recovery.

Gross factor: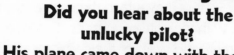

Never underestimate a bug like this. The flu bug is responsible for killing thousands of people throughout the world every year.

Bug Laugh!

Did you hear about the unlucky pilot?
His plane came down with the flu!

Bug Bite

An outbreak of the Spanish Flu in 1918 killed 20 million people all around the world. Worst hit countries were China and India. In the UK, many schools were closed because of the epidemic, and the USA was also badly hit. The US Federal Bureau of Health claimed that during World War One, more US servicemen died from influenza than from wounds.

Bug Laugh!

What do you call an insect with a machine gun?
Baddy long legs!

GIARDIA LAMBLIA

What is it? Pear-shaped bugs that live inside your digestive system.

Grub: This microscopic muncher feeds off the food you eat first.

Case file: Giardia lamblia invade the human body through infected food or water. They attach themselves to the walls of your intestine with their little sucker pads. Once anchored, they relax and wait for their next meal to come along. Although they are relatively harmless, some people will suffer sickness, cramps and diarrhoea as a result.

Gross factor: 🐰🐰🐰🐰🐰

Boy, do these bugs have it easy. They don't even have to look for food – it's all around.

HOOKWORM

What is it? Are you sure you really want to know?

Lives: Starts life quite peacefully buried in moist soil before hatching and deciding to burrow into the skin of innocent passers-by.

Appearance: The Jaws of the worm world. It's thin, long, and uses its teeth to suck human blood.

Grub: Human blood and other fluids the hookworm finds inside your body.

Case file: This nasty piece of work bites its way through human skin, mainly via the foot. Once in the bloodstream, it works its way to your lungs. It then burrows through into your throat where it is swallowed into the intestine – home at last! The hookworm is dangerous to children as it makes their tummies and legs swell up and causes anemia (a shortage of red blood cells). Creepy eruption (horrible itchy red patches) is also caused by hookworm invasions.

Don't panic! Good toilet and water facilities are the best way to beat this bug. Drugs are also available to rid the worm from your system. If you live in a chilly climate, you've nothing to fear – the hookworm larvae only survive in hot tropical places.

Gross factor: 🐛🐛🐛🐛🐛🐛🐛🐛🐛

It's mad, bad and dangerous to know. Some very sick people can get hooked on these worms – they've been found with more than 100 hookworms inside them!

LACTOBACILLUS

What is it? The name given to a group of useful bacteria.

Lives: Trillions are living inside you right now – in your gut and intestine.

Appearance: It cannot be seen with the naked eye. As a bacterium, lactobacillus is among the smallest living things known to man. To view this bug, you need a mighty powerful microscope.

Case file: Lactobacillus may be microscopic but it's vital that it lives in your body if you want to remain fit and healthy. There are different types of helpful bacteria in your body and each performs a different task. Some aid your immune system (your ability to combat disease and harmful bacteria), some help you digest your food, other types produce essential vitamins.

Gross factor: 🐝

Remain calm – without lactobacillus, we would be disease-stricken all the time. Think of the lactobacillus as microscopic warriors, fighting against the bad bacteria to keep you healthy. Lactobacillus, we salute you!

Bug Bite

 Bacteria are a group of single-celled bugs (we are made of trillions of cells). You could fit 1,000 bacteria on this full stop.

 Some types of food and drink contain live bacteria. One healthy yogurt drink boasts that it has 6.5 billion live lactobacillus bacteria in each tiny bottle. How on earth do they squeeze them all in?!

LOUSE

What is it? Small wingless insect with a powerful grip and nasty needle-like mouth.

Lives: On your body, or in your hair, depending on the type of louse it is.

Appearance: This six-legged insect has curved claws on the end of each leg that enable it to grip hair tightly whenever anyone tries to remove it.

Grub: It's a bloodsucker and usually feeds five times a day.

Case file: The two types of louse that live on humans are the body louse and the hair louse. The hair louse lays its eggs (called nits) in your hair while the body louse lays its nits in the seams of your clothes. Both types of louse cause severe itching and rashes. Head lice can be passed on by head to head contact, and you'd be wise not to share combs either. Body lice wander from one item of clothing to another.

Gross factor: 🦟🦟🦟🦟🦟🦟🦟

Lice are treated fairly easily nowadays with the help of specially medicated shampoo, or by getting the itchers out with a very fine tooth comb.

MANGROVE WORM

What is it? Bush tucker ... that's Australian for food from the Outback. Yup, this is the sort of body bug that can help you survive a sticky, starvation-type situation.

Lives: You'll have to seek out your supper. These worms burrow deep inside the trunk of the mangrove tree.

Appearance: Despite its name, the mangrove worm is in

fact a mollusc (a relation of the snail and mussel).

Case file: The Aborigines from Australia eat the mangrove worm raw as a delicacy. Those who have tried the bug say it tastes like crab with a hint of wood. Mmm, sounds mouth-watering, doesn't it?!

Gross factor: 🐛🐛🐛🐛🐛🐛🐛

You would really have to be very lost and very hungry in the Outback to want to eat one of these bugs raw. On the other hand, they might make a tasty addition to the barbecue!

Bug Laugh!

Knock, Knock!
Who's there?
Amos.
Amos who?
A mosquito!

Bug Laugh!

Knock, Knock!
Who's there?
Anna.
Anna who?
And another mosquito!

Bug Bite

The mangrove worm has adapted its shell to use it to bore through timber. Ancient mariners hated the little worm as it made holes in their ships.

PLASMODIUM

What is it? The deadliest parasite bug ever.

Case file: While the mosquito has gained an infamous reputation as a serial killer, this microscopic parasite is the real culprit in question. The mossie carries this parasite which causes malaria. Together, they make a chilling combination of killers, causing half of all human deaths since the Stone Age. Currently, one person in the world dies of malaria every 10 seconds. Isn't it time this parasite took some of the blame?

Fear factor: 🐜🐜🐜🐜🐜🐜🐜🐜🐜🐜

This is the one parasite nobody would want to carry. It's the deadliest bug on earth, bar none.

SCABIES MITE

What is it? A relative of the dust mite. Some people know it as the itch mite. All will be explained …

Lives: The female scabies mite spends its time laying its eggs under your skin.

Appearance: Very hard to see as it is very small, but scientists describe it as "spider-like."

Grub: Once hatched, the larvae of the scabies mite thrive on the liquid your body produces to repair the damage the larvae have already caused. They wriggle away beneath the skin surface, and yes, it is VERY itchy.

Case file: The scabies mite causes a skin disease called scabies. Scabies is very contagious – if you have it, you can

pass it on through skin contact. It can infect any part of
your body from the neck down. Once a scabies mite is
fully grown it heads for your skin's surface where it mates.
The female then digs its burrow in your skin to lay its eggs.

Gross factor:

The scabies mite is a very irritating little invader. Once you
start itching, you just can't stop.

Bug Bite

Doctors treat scabies by using special creams
and lotions that kill the mite. You also have to
wash all your clothes and bed linen so that
the itchy parasite doesn't return.

TAPEWORM

What is it? The X-rated flat worm of the bug world. Read on at your peril, you have been warned.

Lives: Inside the bodies of animals and humans.

Appearance: A tapeworm has no mouth and can grow from anything between 1in to a horrifying 9 yards long!
It has thousands of little segments, similar to an earthworm.

Grub: It eats food absorbed through its body by attaching itself to the intestine (that's inside the stomach) of the animal or person it's living in.

Case file: A tapeworm will get into our bodies if we eat uncooked or undercooked meat, particularly pork and beef, infected with tapeworm larvae. Once inside our bodies, the larvae can grow relatively harmlessly. Yet there have been cases of the young worms growing inside a person's heart, brain and eyes. A tapeworm's eggs are released inside your intestine and make their way through the digestive system before coming out of your bottom when you go to the toilet.

Don't panic! Most folks who have tapeworms won't necessarily have any symptoms. However, you may feel sick, with a loss of appetite and stomach cramps.

Bug Laugh!

How do you discover the length of a tapeworm?
Use a tape measure!

TSETSE FLY

What is it? Flying sleeping sickness carrier.

Lives: This disease carrying tsetse fly is only found in Africa.

Case file: The tsetse fly carries a microscopic parasite and is spread to humans when the fly sucks human blood. The fly has large biting mouthparts which it sinks into its victim's skin, passing the parasite into the blood stream. People become so exhausted by the disease that they can hardly move – hence the name, sleeping sickness.

Gross factor: 🐜🐜🐜🐜🐜🐜🐜

In Africa, the population would sleep a lot easier at night if they didn't have to worry about this dangerous little pest.

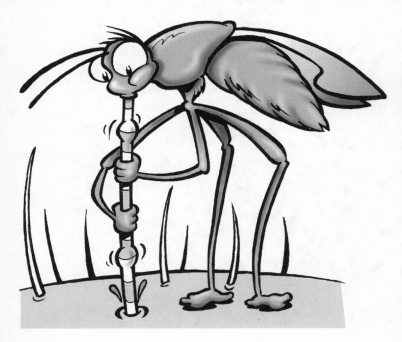

Big bugs

Some bugs seem to be
scary just because of their sheer
size and scale. This chapter is all about
the giant-sized beasties that strike fear into
the hearts of humankind. OK, so some of them
are purely fictional, we must admit. But that
doesn't stop us from worrying about 'em!

EDGAR

What is it? The huge alien bug that nearly destroyed planet earth in top movie Men In Black.

Lives: He comes from an unknown galaxy.

Appearance: Edgar is able to disguise himself as a human before revealing his true horrific identity in all his bug-like glory to top-secret government MiB Agent Jay.

Case file: Arrived to cause death and destruction by forcing aliens to attack Earth after Edgar's murder of the alien ambassador. Thanks to the heroic action of MiB agents Jay and Kay, who managed to blow Edgar up, the wholesale destruction of Earth was avoided. Phew.

Fear factor:

Enormous and nasty with a healthy appetite for MiB agents, Edgar's weakness was his love for Earth's bug life and his temper when anyone hurt his smaller Earth cousins. But can you really fear any bug that dances like THAT?!

GIANT SPIDER

What is it? A fictional alien spider from the seventies' sci-fi TV series Doctor Who.

Lives: On planet Metebelis 3, a human colony found in another distant galaxy.

Appearance: Huge eight-legged rubbery thing that seems to crawl without moving its legs.

Grub: Unsure, possibly humans.

Weapons: The giant spider is able to take over humans by jumping on their backs and staying there – invisibly – while controlling them through telepathy.

Case file: The giant spider worshiped a huge mutated spider called the Great One. The giant spider's mission was to recover a blue crystal that the Time Lord Doctor Who had pinched from Metebelis 3. Its mission failed when the Great One used the blue crystal to increase her powers, but instead blew the whole giant spider colony to kingdom come. Shame.

Fear factor: 🕷

Thanks to Doctor Who, the giant spider is no more. Mind you, we might all fancy our chances against this rubbery and unconvincing alien.

Bug Laugh!
What do you call two spiders who have just got married? Newly-webs!

GOLIATH BEETLE

What is it? The big daddy of the beetles and one of the largest creatures in the bug world.

Lives: Only to be found in Africa, with a large number thundering around the rainforests near the equator.

Appearance: Six-legged armored flying machine. It can grow up to 5in long, but its bulk is impressive and it is

easily one of the heaviest bugs around.

Grub: A fully-grown goliath beetle has a sweet tooth and will enjoy fruit and sugary sap from injured trees.

Weapons: Its bulk and thick outer wings. The male also has a horn to fight other guys when out to impress the girls.

Case file: As baby larvae, the goliath beetle plays a vital role in the upkeep of the rainforests by eating decaying plants and leaves. When it flies, this beetle is so large it is said to sound like a helicopter in flight.

Fear Factor: 🪲 🪲

Definitely a case of a creature whose bark is worse than its bite. A real gentle giant!

Bug Laugh!

How do beetles walk their babies? In a buggy!

GOLDEN ORB-WEB

What is it? The world's biggest web–weaving spider.

Case file: The biggest web spun by a golden orb-web spider was found in India and measured 1.5 yards in circumference. It had supporting lines spun from silk that measured 6 yards in length!

Strange but true! Golden orb-webs produce the strongest of all spider silks!

Fear Factor: 🪲 🪲 🪲 🪲 🪲 🪲

Just keep away from that web, OK?

HERCULES BEETLE

What is it? The longest beetle in the world.

Strange but true! Measuring up to 7in long, the hercules beetle's huge horn makes up more than half its length. This beetle can be found in Central and South America.

Fear factor:

Looks can be very deceptive. It would run a mile rather than tackle you.

HORNET

What is it? A super large wasp.

Lives: The hornet is a pretty impressive home maker and lives in large paper nests which it makes by chewing up wood and plant stems. Usually about the size of a soccer ball, these nests can be found hanging from trees or even tucked away in quiet parts of buildings.

Appearance: What distinguishes a hornet and wasp from a bee is its thin waist, but it still has that distinctive striped yellow and black body.

Case file: Like bees, it is a social insect and lives in a colony of other hornets that is divided into workers, males and the leader of the pack – the queen. Equipped with a sting, the hornet is considered slightly more nervous than the bee, and is therefore more likely to sting.

Fear factor: >ᵇᵉ->ᵇᵉ->ᵇᵉ->ᵇᵉ->ᵇᵉ- The hornet is just as feared by us as the bee and wasp. In fact, a lot of people can't tell the difference and think they are all the same bug. But its reputation as a flying pest hell-bent on stinging people is not based on fact.

KATYDID

What is it? The bug that makes a BIG noise – all night long!

Lives: The noisiest variety of katydid can be found in the rainforests of the Amazon in South America. Some are also found in the United States.

Appearance: Close relation to the cricket and the grasshopper. The katydid is distinguished by mega feelers that help it feel around at night when it is most active.

Weapons: This bug can be easy prey for snakes and small mammals, but its ingenious way of disguising itself as a motionless leaf saves its skin on many occasions.

Grub: Leaves, stems, flowers and fruit of various plants.

Case file: This noisy bug makes its sound by rubbing the base of its front legs together. Believe it or not, this unattractive sound is the male's mating call! Katydids play a crucial part in the Amazonian life cycle – as well as eating plant life, they also provide an important link in the food chain as they make up the staple diet of monkeys, birds and bats.

Fear factor: 🐛 🐛

But you will always know when it's about – that racket will keep you up all night!

PRAYING MANTIS

What is it? The predator bug whose female likes to snack on the male during breeding.

Lives: Amongst leaves, flowers, shrubs and trees in the tropics and sunny temperate parts of the globe.

Appearance: One species of praying mantis found in Sri Lanka reaches 10in in length. Very hard to spot as the praying mantis is well adapted to it surroundings. But it stands still for hours with its forelegs held out before it, waiting patiently …

Grub: Any bug that unwittingly comes near the patient mantis' powerful grip. Quick as lightning, the mantis will strike with its forelegs before sinking its equally powerful jaws into its prey.

Case file: The female praying mantis is renowned for eating her male partner during mating … apparently she just cannot resist biting his head off! A hungry praying mantis has been known to hold one victim with its forelegs while devouring another. Jeez, this is one hungry bug!

Fear factor:

The praying mantis is a fascinating bug that you just can't help admiring. Just be grateful it's not human size – now THAT would be scary!

Bug Bite

 A mantis will develop outgrowths from its body to look like twigs, grass or leaves. This helps it hide from predators and fool prey.

 The praying mantis gets its name from a Greek word meaning prophet. It also looks like it is deep in prayer when waiting for prey.

 Many martial arts schools in the East are named in this bug's honor.

PRAYING MANTIS ALIEN

What is it? A super-size alien, supposedly spotted in the USA back in 1973.

Appearance: Black insects standing 2 yards high.

Lives: Anybody's guess!

Strange but true! Mike Shea of Maryland, USA, was driving to meet a friend when a brilliant white light blinded him. He then says he saw a huge, silent, saucer-like craft. While driving away, he claims to have seen four further praying mantis aliens before being blinded again. Next thing Mike knew, he was on board with the aliens taking hair and skin samples. He was then returned to his car.

Fear factor: 🐜🐜🐜

A UFO encounter with alien bugs is pretty hair-raising. This, on the other hand, sounds about as likely as Mickey Mouse running for President.

SPACE SLUG

What is it? Absolutely huge slug that grows to more than 900 yards long in Star Wars movie The Empire Strikes Back.

Lives: Within asteroids in a galaxy far, far away.

Case file: Han Solo had a close encounter with one while flying the Millennium Falcon. It is a silicon-based bug that lives on the mineral content of asteroids.

Fear factor: 🐜🐜🐜🐜🐜🐜

Even in the safety of the fastest ship in the galaxy, you could end up as slug supper.

STAG BEETLE

What is it? Battling beetle.

Appearance: Big and black, with huge jaws or horns.

Case file: Its name comes from the male of the species who has two large horns that look like the antlers of a real stag. Male stag beetles fight to protect their territory and a battle between two beetles is a pretty fearsome affair. Each will grapple with the other, locking horns until one lifts the other and dumps it to the ground. If the loser is unfortunate enough to land on its back, it spells disaster as this cumbersome bug could end up as the main course for some particularly peckish ants.

Fear factor: 🥊🥊🥊🥊🥊

Beetles aren't that scary. Big beetles are.

STICK INSECT

What is it? The peaceful king of camouflage.

Lives: Motionless on the leaves and branches of trees and shrubs in warm tropical countries.

Grub: Strictly vegetarian, it munches on berries and leaves.

Appearance: Very thin and long. It is an expert in disguise and you'd probably go bug-eyed trying to pick one out.

Case file: As the stick insect sheds its skin continuously, it grows at a very quick rate in just a few months. A stick insect can regrow any damaged or lost legs, all it takes is a few skin sheddings. "Stickies" make popular pets – they're gentle, need little space, and are very cheap to keep. On the downside, you can't hug them, take them for walks or ask them to fetch the newspaper.

Fear factor:

The stick insect may look slightly odd, but it's the gentle giant of the bug world.

Bug Bite

 One of the greenest bugs around, the stick insect even eats the skin it sheds!

The Pharnacia kirbyi stick insect is the longest recorded insect in the world measuring in at more than 18in long!

TARANTULA

What is it? An arachnid. One of the world's largest – and most infamous – spiders.

Lives: It can live in a burrow or hide out in trees. Tarantulas are found in south-west USA, but the largest live in the jungles of South America.

Appearance: A big, hairy spider that can measure up to 10in long. Yup, that big!

Grub: Small rodents, birds and lizards. It has even been known to snack on pit vipers and rattlesnakes. In the early 1920s, a captive tarantula killed and chomped its way through two frogs, a small rattlesnake, and a highly poisonous Jararaca snake in just four days!

Weapons: A tarantula has large fangs that deliver a venomous bite to kill its prey. It spins no web, so relies on speed when hunting. The tarantula also has an impressive secret weapon in its arsenal – it can fling thousands of microscopic hairs at an attacker by rubbing its hind legs. And boy, are these itchy!

Case file: Powerful stomach juices dissolve the flesh of its prey. A tarantula can turn a mouse into a pile of bones and hair in 36 hours – just by sucking.

Strange but true: This huge hairy spider can live for more than 20 years.

Fear factor: 🐜🐜🐜🐜🐜🐜

Despite the sight of a tarantula turning the biggest bug lover weak at the knees, it rarely attacks humans unless provoked. Some spider fanatics even keep them as pets.

Bug Bite

The tarantula gets its name from the Italian town of Taranto. People once thought that the tarantula's bite gave you tarantism, an illness that caused folk to run around jumping up and down making strange noises (sounds like break dancing!). According to superstition, the best cure was a strange Italian folk dance called the tarantella!

TROPICAL EMPEROR

What is it? One of the world's largest scorpions. Also known as the imperial scorpion.

Lives: West Africa.

Appearance: Yellow in color. The male of the species can grow up to 7in long. One tropical emperor captured in Sierra Leone in 1977 measured a whopping 9.5in!

Grub: Insects and rodents.

Weapons: A pair of pincers and a tail with a venomous sting. But size isn't everything…

Fear factor: 🐜🐜🐜🐜🐜

Fearsome in appearance, it packs little punch. Its sting is the equivalent of a bee sting, although occasionally an allergic reaction to the sting has caused the victim to die.

THEM!

What is it? Giant man-munching sci-fi movie ants.

Lives: In the desert of New Mexico, before making their way to Los Angeles.

Appearance: 7 yards long. Unrealistic, but in the black and white 1950s it was thought to be pretty convincing.

Grub: Us (gulp!).

Weapons: Its huge mouth, capable of tearing through metal and human flesh in a matter of minutes.

Case file: Them! were discovered by two New Mexico state patrolmen after secret atomic testing in the desert had spawned a colony of killer ants. After investigation by FBI officer James Arness, and the father and daughter scientist team Edmund Gwenn and Joan Weldon, they realized that if the queen ant mated the world would be overrun by giant insects. Thankfully, the nest was located to the Los Angeles drainage system and the ants were torched by the US Army, armed with flame throwers. No more Them!

Fear factor: 🐜🐜🐜🐜🐜

Them! had people fleeing from cinemas in 1954. Nowadays, the "special effects" would have audiences howling with laughter.

ZARBI

What is it? An alien ant from the Doctor Who series.

Lives: On the planet Vortis.

Appearance: A giant black ant with human legs and one very unstable looking head.

Weapons: A sinister waving of its arms and legs.

Case file: The peace-loving zarbi were enslaved by the evil animus upon its invasion of Vortis. The animus then forced the zarbi to oppress the other native of Vortis, the intelligent mentoptra. Following the destruction of animus by Doctor Who and the mentoptra, the zarbi returned to their former peace-loving ways.

Fear factor: 🐜🐜🐜🐜🐜

Despite being painfully stupid, the possibility of the zarbi's head falling off at any moment was a real danger.

Flying bugs

For those who get
squeamish about bugs, it seems
there's nothing quite so annoying as the
ones that buzz about and flap around. They
plague our picnics, spoil our summers and
generally make a nuisance of themselves. But
there's also a bevy of beautiful flying bugs who
enhance our environment. Read on!

BIRDWING BUTTERFLY

What is it? The Queen Alexandra's birdwing butterfly (to give it its full name) has the biggest wingspan of any living bug. Once seen, never forgotten.

Case file: The birdwing can only be found in Papua New Guinea, and its wingspan can reach 11in from one tip to the other!

Strange but true! You'd be lucky to see this fella – it's very rare and lives up to 40 yards above ground in vine leaves.

Fear factor:

An awesome sight to behold, but nothing to interrupt your sweet dreams at night.

BOMBARDIER BEETLE

What is it? The bug with the exploding bottom!

Case file: Bombardier beetles have one of the most remarkable defence systems in the bug world. If attacked, the bombardier can produce a nasty explosion – a hot, skin-blistering poisonous gas is released from its rear end that would cause any would-be predator to back off! Quite

Bug Bite

The bombardier's gas reaches a scorching temperature of 100°C. Hot or what?!

how it manages this without blowing itself up is a mystery.

Fear factor: 🐜🐜🐜
Rest assured, the bombardier beetle will
only use its artillery if under attack…

DAMSELFLY

What is it? Close relative of the dragonfly.

Lives: Around water, just like its buzzin' cousin.

Appearance: Brilliant blue and green.

Case file: As expert fliers, damselflies' great claim to fame
is that they can mate while still in the air. Show offs.

Strange but true! You can spot the difference between
dragonflies and damselflies by their wings. When a damsel
rests, it holds its wings over its back. A dragonfly, on the
other hand, will spread its wings out. Damselflies' bodies
are also more slender and more fragile.

Fear factor: 🐜🐜
Damselflies are dainty darlings of the bug world. Nothing
scary there, huh?

Bug Bite

Damsel and dragonflies are real old-timers of
the bug world. They've been around for more
than 300 million years!

DRAGONFLY

What is it? Mesmerizing flying insect.

Lives: Seen hovering gracefully above ponds and streams.

Appearance: Majestic. As well as having an incredibly sleek body, the dragonfly comes in a whole rainbow of colors: red, green or blue. If the sun catches its wings, it gives the impression that it's glowing.

Grub: Carnivorous, and will enjoy tucking into any small bug, even when in full flight.

Bug Bite

 In top gear, the dragonfly can reach speeds of almost 60mph.

Case file: The dragonfly has four wings that are very frail and almost transparent. You may see a dragonfly perched on a lily, but it cannot actually walk. A fully grown dragonfly will live for only a few weeks, although it lives in a pond as a nymph (baby) for up to five years.

Fear factor: 👓 👓

Harmless to humans, it's still a bug we all know and love when strolling next to a pond on a hot summer's day.

Bug Laugh!

Why do bees have sticky hair? Because they insist on using honeycombs!

Bug Laugh!

What time is it when a fly and a flea pass each other? Fly past flea!

Bug Bite

Moths and bugs have some of the weirdest names in the bug world.

Try these for size: the death's head hawk moth, the green banded ohe ohe leaf-roller moth, and the pale hockey stick sailer!

EMPEROR MOTH

What is it? The best nose in the business.

Case file: The emperor moth has a clever form of defence from predators, as its hindwings have "eye spots." If frightened by an enemy – usually a bird – it flashes its "eyes" to frighten off its would-be predator!

Strange but true! The male emperor moth has the most acute sense of smell in the whole animal kingdom. It can sniff out a female emperor moth 7 miles away!

Fear factor: 🐜🐜🐜🐜
With an amazing sense of smell, unrivaled in the insect world, the Emperor is a bug that's surely not to be sniffed at!

GYPSY MOTH

What is it? Well-known moth.

Lives: Woodlands and orchards.

Appearance: The gypsy moth is a master of disguise. Up against a tree, its patterned brown and gray coloring makes it very hard to spot.

Grub: The gypsy moth caterpillar has a bit of a reputation as a pest and has been known to strip trees bare of their leaves and fruit with its ravenous appetite.

Case file: The gypsy moth caterpillar's appetite for foliage and fruit will eventually kill a tree. Gypsy moths have a particularly destructive taste for the oak. Only the male gypsy moth tends to fly, though – the female prefers to look after her eggs.

Fear factor:

Although if you happen to be an oak tree, that might increase the fear factor three-fold.

HOUSE FLY

What is it? A two-winged flying insect.

Lives: In your house and on your food, if you don't keep your eyes peeled. When they go outside, flies are found in rubbish bins, compost heaps and other hang-outs too gross to mention.

Appearance: They're usually too quick to get a good look at them. Black body with a set of wings either side. Two big bug eyes.

Weapons: Themselves. Flies are a disease's dream date – they carry germs inside their bodies, on their mouth and in their hair. Germ-infested, you might say.

Case file: The buzzing a fly makes is the sound of its wings beating. A house fly is among the fastest insects known to man. It can beats its wings 200 times a second, reaching speeds of up to 45mph. Now here's the really nasty stuff. A fly can't bite or chew food, so it uses its tube-like mouth to spit and vomit on its chow. When it's all nice and gooey, they suck it up, happily spreading germs all over your dinner in the process! If you eat food that a fly has been snacking on, you could get diarrhoea, food poisoning, or typhoid.

Fear factor:

House flies are more of a nuisance than a danger but remember to give this buzzing bug a good swat if it looks like landing on your food. It's a filthy beast.

Bug Laugh!

Waiter! Waiter! What's this fly doing in my soup?
Looks like the breast-stroke to me, sir...

Bug Bite

Flies have hairy feet that are covered in a sticky substance that helps them to climb up windows and mirrors. Sounds like they'd make great window cleaners!

JUMPING SPIDER

What is it? An eight-legged Olympian.

Lives: This spider loves soaking up the rays on a rock in warm countries such as Australia.

Appearance: A jumping spider has shorter, stockier legs than most other spiders, and a chunky, compact body. Some are even called "ant-like spiders" as they look like an ant, and can mix happily with ants without being attacked.

Weapons: Its excellent eyesight and its ability to pounce on unsuspecting prey.

Case file: A jumping spider is described as the tiger of the spider world for its ability to sneak up on its prey (usually a juicy fly or insect) and surprise it with one quick leap. It then sinks its jaws into its prey to kill it. A jumping spider also attaches a line of silk onto a tree or wall before jumping to make sure it doesn't fall to the floor. This eight-legged hunter has three rows of eyes that allow it to see in every direction, even behind itself!

Fear factor: 🕷🕷

Despite looking slightly menacing, a jumping spider is actually handy for ridding your household of pesky pests.

Bug Bite

 A jumping spider can leap between 3 and 6 in.

LOCUST

What is it? Phenomenal crop destroyer that flies around in huge plagues. Features heavily in nasty biblical episodes.

Lives: In African countries, the Middle East and parts of the United States of America.

Appearance: Big head and large eyes, with long hind legs for jumping and four wings for flying. Oh, and what a mouth!

Grub: Fields of rice, corn, wheat ... basically any vegetation that's going.

Strange but true! In 1988, one locust swarm in Sudan was measured at 94 miles long.

Case file: A common locust swarm can contain 48,000 bugs per square mile. Given that a locust can eat its own weight each day, that would mean a swarm is capable of eating the equivalent of what 10 elephants or 2,500 people will eat in a single day. An attack by a plague on crops can leave poor farmers in African countries such as Mozambique and Tanzania close to starvation. Controlling these pests isn't easy either – some insecticides can do more harm than good.

Fear Factor: 🐜🐜🐜🐜🐜🐜🐜🐜

These greedy menaces show no mercy. They leave some of the world's most vulnerable people facing starvation and ruin.

Bug Bite

In Africa, there's one group that's determined to get its own back on these greedy bugs. The nomadic Tuaregs of the Sahara love to tuck in to a dish of fried locusts with dates! They also grind the locusts down to produce what they believe is a magical powder. The Tuaregs claim it protects them from the evils of the desert.

MENOPTRA

What is it? A harmless alien butterfly.

Lives: It's native to the planet Vortis.

Appearance: A Hallowe'en costume gone wrong or an actor dressed as a giant butterfly.

Weapons: None – it's harmless!

Case file: The menoptra, led by Captain Hilio, were an advanced and noble butterfly people before the animus invaded Vortis and forced them to seek refuge. The menoptra joined forces with the Time Lord Doctor Who and their wingless underground cousins, the optera, to rid Vortis of the animus and free its slaves, the ant-like Zarbi.

Fear factor:

It was a lot easier to laugh at these ridiculous creatures than fear them.

PAINTED LADY

What is it? Traveling butterfly.

Grub: The painted lady caterpillar likes to munch on thistles. And thistles. And more thistles.

Case file: Like the monarch butterfly, the orange and brown colored painted lady sets off on an incredible migration – over 1800 miles – from North Africa to Europe before returning back to Africa when the weather turns chilly.

Fear factor:

This lady's incredible journey demands respect, not fear.

Bug Laugh!

Why wasn't the butterfly allowed to the dance?
Because it was a moth-ball!

Bug Laugh!

How do you start a bug race?
One-two-flea GO!

Bug Laugh!

Why do bees hum?
They've forgotten the words!

Bug Bite

The painted lady is found all over the world, hence its other name – the cosmopolitan.

PONDSKATER

What is it? The water walker.

Lives: On the surface of ponds, skimming along the water's "skin," scavenging for food.

Grub: Any hapless bug that finds itself drowning.

Case file: This clever little scavenger uses its middle and rear pairs of legs as oars, while its front legs come in handy for capturing prey. They know when grub's up – the giveaway ripples on the surface of the pond are a sure sign that there's an insect in trouble – and next thing you know is, it's suppertime!

Fear factor:
Unless you're very tiny and can't swim, the pondskater is pretty harmless, really.

RED ADMIRAL

What is it? One of the world's most popular butterflies.

Lives: Thankfully, this beautiful flyer likes to be seen in all the American continent, Europe, New Zealand, northern Africa and Asia. A real worldwide star.

Appearance: Strikingly decked out in black with red bands and white spots. Underneath, a red admiral is dark brown with black and blue patches. Stunning.

Grub: As a caterpillar, it's happy to tuck into a bunch of stinging nettles. But when it transforms into an adult, the red admiral prefers tree sap and decaying fruit. It will still drink a flower's nectar if it has to, though.

Case file: The red admiral migrates around and will hibernate come the winter. It is a common sight in gardens and can be found anywhere there are flowers.

Fear factor:

The only thing you need fear is that you may never see a red admiral again. Numbers are dwindling.

THE WASP

Who is she? Janet Van Dyne – crime-busting super hero and part of the early Avengers alongside Ant-Man, the Incredible Hulk, the Mighty Thor and Iron Man.

Lives: Comic book land, USA.

Appearance: Looks rather like a modern day Tinker Bell in a flashy red and yellow outfit.

Weapons: Her speed, feisty personality and good looks.

Case file: After meeting Henry Pym (aka Ant-Man) after her scientist father was murdered, Henry made Janet his crime-busting partner. Pym gave Janet the power to shrink herself down, and also gave her the ability to grow wings at insect size – hence her name the Wasp. In the 1980s, she became one of the Avengers' most effective leaders.

Fear factor:

Hey, this bug's a superhero! Apart from her good looks and flying skills, the Wasp was an inspired leader and a major force in the fight against crime. She showed real Girl Power way before the Spice Girls popped onto the scene. Or should that be Wasp Power?

Bug Laugh!

What's a wasp's favorite music?
Anything by Sting!

Bug Laugh!

Where do you take injured wasps?
To a waspital!

How do bees get from place to place?
By buzz!

Buddy bugs

Not all bugs are baddies.
In fact, some bugs do more than
their fair share to make our world
a happier and healthier place to live. So
before you prepare to squish that bug, make
sure you familiarize yourself with this chapter.
One day, you may just need that bug!

THE BEATLES

Who are they? They were the greatest pop band in the world … ever. Unless you prefer the Backstreet Boys.

Lives: Formed in Liverpool, England in the 60s, before going their separate ways in 1970.

Appearance: Four likely lads: John Lennon, Paul McCartney, Ringo Starr, and George Harrison, first spotted in Liverpool's Cavern Club.

Case file: The Beatles' first record, Love Me Do, was released in 1962. Almost overnight, the world was seized by Beatlemania. Symptoms included continuous screaming, crying and pulling out hair in the presence of the fab four. Records like Let It Be, Help!, and Penny Lane sold in their thousands throughout the world.

Hero factor: 🪲🪲🪲🪲🪲🪲🪲🪲🪲
The screams of those devoted fans could make the hairs on the back of your neck stand up. Frighteningly famous.

BEETLEBORGS

What are they? Three kids who were granted their wish to become comic book heroes, the Big Bad Beetleborgs.

Lives: Charterville.

Appearance: Multi-colored medieval knights who can move at the speed of lightning.

Weapons: Each Beetleborg has a different skill and weapon. The Red Striker has super strength, activated by popping her knuckles and uses the Striker Blaster and sonic laser.

The Blue Stinger can move objects about just by nodding his head, and carries the stinger blade and the stinger drill. The Green Hunter can run extremely fast by snapping his fingers – and that hunter claw comes in handy too.

Case file: The Beetleborgs were created after youngsters Jo McCormick, Drew McCormick and Roland Williams were locked in a haunted house called Hillhurst. After unleashing a funtastic phasm called Flabber, they were granted one wish and all decided to transform into Beetleborgs. Unfortunately, silly old Flabber also released the evil Vexor and his Magnavors. After a series of battles, the Beetleborgs finally defeated Vexor and packed him off back to comic book world forever. However, once the villainous Crustaceans turned up on the scene, the Beetleborgs needed new weapons, armor and powers … and that's how the Beetleborgs Metallix were born.

Hero factor: 🐝🐝🐝🐝🐝🐝🐝

Flash, brash and ready to save their home town, the Beetleborgs are bugs you wouldn't want to mess with.

BUMBLE BEE

What is it? Large, stocky bee that pollinates flowers.

Lives: All over the world flying from blossom to blossom during the summer. The bumble bee lives in a colony.

Appearance: Resembles the honey bee but the bumble is longer and broader. It also has a thick covering of yellow and black hair.

Grub: Nectar from flowers.

Weapons: Its sting. Unlike the honey bee, the bumble can sting again and again without dying. However, it will only sting if it feels seriously threatened.

Case file: Bumble bees do not live in hives, but make a nest in holes in the ground or in grassy banks. Every year a queen bumble will start a new colony by producing young worker bees to find food. The queen's next task is to rear new queen bees and drone bees to mate in the fall. Once the new queens have mated, they will fly off to hibernate for the winter. The old queen and workers die. Sounds like a tough old life, eh?

Hero factor: 🐝🐝🐝🐝🐝🐝

The poison of a bumble bee sting can be painful, but these guys are busy. Give 'em a break.

Bug Laugh!

What do you call a modest bee? A humble bumble!

Bug Bite

Bumble bees are important as they help pollinate flowers by carrying pollen on their bodies from one flower to the next.

EARTHWORM

What is it? The gardener's best buddy.

Lives: The earthworm can be found burrowing deep in the soil. Tends to come to the surface after a bout of rain.

Appearance: Come on! Everyone knows what an earthworm looks like, don't they? It's kind of wormy and wriggles a lot!

What does it do? Cleans the soil so that it's fertile and better for growing things.

Grub: Leaves and dirt which it pushes into its body (sadly, it has no teeth).

Case file: Earthworms are underground farmers, turning the soil over like a plough. In a small patch of land, there can be more than a million earthworms eating 10 tons of

109

leaves, stems, and dead roots a year, and turning over 40 tons of soil. Even an earthworm's pooh is good for the soil, replacing valuable nutrients. The skin of an earthworm feels slimy to the touch as it needs to be moist for the worm to breathe properly.

Hero factor: 🐛🐛🐛🐛🐛🐛🐛

People just don't give these little critters credit for keeping soil clean. And, no, wriggly worms are not scary!

Bug Laugh!

How do you tell which end of the worm is its head?
Tickle its middle and see which end smiles!

Bug Bite

Bug Bite! Famous scientist Charles Darwin studied the earthworm for 39 years and said: "It may be doubted whether there are many other animals in the world which have played so important a part in the history of the world."

Ancient Egyptian queen Cleopatra was a fan as well, and declared earthworms sacred creatures. She wasn't so fond of snakes though!

LEECH

What is it? Probably the ugliest bug in the creepy-crawlie kingdom.

Lives: Anywhere dark and damp, like the moist soils of tropical jungles. Some even like to wallow in shallow streams and lakes.

Appearance: A long, squishy snail without its home. Leeches are red, brown or black with spots and stripes, and have round suckers at each end. And once they're attached to us humans, they're not easily dislodged.

Grub: Like to eat decaying animals and plants, although a certain number of them have developed a taste for blood.

Case file: A leech can stretch or contract its body to be either short and stubby, or long and thin. Leech saliva contains a chemical substance that prevents blood from clotting. In medieval times, leeches were used as "cures" for certain illnesses as it was believed that sucking out (or "letting," as it was called) some of the patient's blood would help them recover. A couple of leeches would be let loose on the body and left to suck away. Yeeurgh!

Strange but true: Today, medicinal leeches are still used. Doctors use them to prevent scabs forming on wounds, especially following delicate operations such as plastic surgery, or after severed fingers or hands have been re-attached. This helps the wound heal from the inside outwards – and that's very important for delicate repairs.

Hero factor:

OK, they may help medical science, but have you seen what these suckers look like?!

MAGGOT

What is it? This limbless larva of the fly is nothing short of a medical miracle. Yes, it really is.

Lives: Usually a maggot will live buried in food, but specially bred, sterilized varieties are found in hospitals too. Oh yes, and you'll normally find a few tucked away in an angler's bag?

Appearance: White in color, this legless bug is best described as a short, stubby caterpillar. It moves around by wriggling or flipping its body.

Case file: The maggot has made a bit of a comeback in modern medicine as it can clean wounds effectively. It does this by eating bacteria found on a cut or sore, and stops it becoming infected. Just spread your maggots over the injured area, cover them with a bandage, and let them weave their magic for three days. Whereas some bacteria have become resistant to antibiotics, others will always lose the battle with these clever little bugs – well you can't put up much of a fight against a munching maggot, can you?! And some doctors even believe a maggot has its own helpful secretions that help heal and numb a wound.

Hero factor: 🐛🐛🐛🐛🐛🐛🐛

Forget George Clooney – for top notch emergency aid, it's the maggot every time.

Bug Laugh!

What's worse than finding a maggot in your apple?
Finding half a maggot in your apple!

ROBUG

What is it? An eight-legged futuristic robot.

Lives: In nuclear fuel sites.

What does it do? This bug is designed for picking up and moving dangerous substances in a nuclear reactor. Has an attachable arm that can help it reach injured people in case of a radioactive accident.

Appearance: Looks like a big mechanical spider. It's 4 feet long, 2 feet wide and 2 feet tall. Weighing in at 120lb, the Robug is made of lightweight carbon fiber.

Intelligence: Robug is controlled by a highly sophisticated computer via a data cable.

Case file: Suction pads enable the Robug to climb up walls and even ceilings as well as dragging loads of up to 250lb if needed. This robot is also fitted with video cameras, a laser range finder, and a Geiger counter to measure radiation leaks.

Hero factor: 🐛🐛🐛🐛🐛🐛

This powerful bug will save the day – and even the odd life – in the event of a nuclear accident.

SACRED SCARAB

What is it? A bright, golden beetle once worshiped by the Ancient Egyptians. Scarab is a large group of beetles; the scared scarab is known as scarabaeus sacer.

Lives: In Ancient Egypt, the scarab symbolized resurrection and everlasting life.

Appearance: Because of its oval shape and golden color, the Ancient Egyptians believed it was one of the forms their sun god assumed.

Grub: Err … how can we put this – dung.

Case file: When the beetle rolled a ball of dung, the Egyptians thought it symbolized the Earth revolving – with the scarab representing the sun. The beetle was carved on to jewelry, precious stones and often turned up in mummies' tombs. It also represented resurrection and immortality. The Ancient Egyptians would remove the heart of a dead person and replace it with a carved jeweled scarab during the embalming process.

Hero factor: 🐞🐞🐞

Ancient Egyptians thought the scarab beetle was to be hero worshiped. Nowadays we are less impressed by the activities of dung beetles. Still, look good on jewelry...

SILKWORM

What is it? The pampered weaver of the bug world.

Lives: In special farms where it's treated like royalty. The silkworm's every need is catered for – even protecting it from flies and diseases.

Appearance: Starts life as a white caterpillar before changing into a large, white moth about 2in long.

What does it do? Produces silk – an expensive, shiny fiber that's super-soft on the skin, and used to make luxurious clothes. It's expensive as it's strong and elastic, and those farms don't come cheap, either.

Grub: A silkworm's favorite food is mulberry tree leaves.

Case file: Silk is produced when the silkworm caterpillar forces two fine strands of goo out of the small pores in its head. When the ooze turns solid, it becomes silk. The tiny silkworm produces the silk thread to weave its cocoons before turning into a moth. On a silk farm, millions of silkworms are kept in special trays filled with mulberry tree leaves so they can chomp away happily.

Hero factor: 🐛🐛🐛🐛🐛🐛🐛🐛

Considered the most treasured insect in the world, especially by those who like to sport shiny shirts.

Bug Bite

 Silk (also known as the queen of fibers) was discovered by the Chinese more than 4,000 years ago. According to Chinese legend, the silkworm's wondrous weaving was discovered in 2700BC by the emperor's wife, Xilingshi. She was hot on the trail of the silkworm after she discovered that some nasty little bug had been chowing down on her precious mulberry trees. Of course, once she'd got her first pair of silk pajamas, she soon forgave the little wrigglers!

 The Chinese guarded the secret of the silkworm for thousands of years. Anyone suspected of giving the game away faced disgrace and even death!

SPIDER-MAN

Who is he? A very famous super-hero. His real-life alter ego is Peter Parker, but that's classified information – we don't want that leaked to The Daily Bugle where he works.

Lives: New York City.

Appearance: Wears a red and blue figure-hugging body suit covered in black web shapes and a mask.

Weapons: The powers of a spider: superhuman strength, the ability to climb walls plus an extrasensory "spider sense" alerting him to impending danger. Spider-Man also has a sticky webbing that he shoots from both his wrists that allows him to swing from building to building. It also comes in handy for wrapping up criminals.

Case file: Spider-Man first appeared in 1962 when 15-year-old Peter Parker was bitten by a radioactive spider during a school trip to an atomic research lab. Peter combined his crime fighting antics as Spider-Man with a career working as a freelance news photographer for The Daily Bugle. Spider-Man has a whole host of baddies to battle including the Green Goblin, Doctor Octopus, Mysterio, the Kingpin and the Sandman.

Hero factor: 🕷🕷🕷🕷🕷🕷🕷🕷🕷

"Spider-Man, Spider-Man does whatever a spider can!" Well, with radioactive blood, that's no great surprise...

Bug Laugh!
What do you call a spider with no legs?
A currant!

Z

Who is he? Z-4195 (or Z for short) is the ant hero of the smash hit animated movie, Antz.

Lives: In Antopia, which looks like a tatty old picnic site piled high with litter to you and me.

Appearance: Comes across as a skinny wimp with a weedy voice, especially when facing the deadly termites. But underneath, Z's a real hero when you need him.

Case file: Unhappy misfit Z wants to be more than just an ordinary worker ant, especially after meeting and falling in love with Princess Bala, the queen ant in waiting. With the help of his tough soldier ant buddy Weaver, Z reluctantly leads a colony-wide revolt against boredom. It's also a blow for the ant colony's military leader, who is plotting to wipe out billions of ordinary ants like Z.

Hero factor: 🐜🐜🐜🐜🐜🐜

Z may not look like your typical hero at first glance, but when his back is against the wall, this is one little bug you know you can count on.

The Bug Quiz

Now you know everything about bugs, right?
Well let's just check and see how much attention you've
been paying...

BAD BUGS

1 How many people are
struck down by malaria
every year?
   a **100 million**
   b **200 million**
   c **300 million**

2 What's the world's
deadliest scorpion?

3 An anti-venom for the
funnel-web spider bite
was invented in 1980.
True or false?

4 Who did Eddie Brock
turn into?

5 When will the Millennium
Bug strike?
   a **midnight on
      31 December 1999**
   b **1 January 2001**
   c **31 December 2000**

6 The black widow has
been known to spin
webs across toilet seats.
True or false?

BODACIOUS BUGS

7 Pop star Adam Ant had a hit with a song called Ant Melody.
True or false?

8 Why do bees make a buzzing sound?

9 How far do Monarch butterflies migrate?
a **20 miles**
b **200 miles**
c **2000 miles**

10 What do spitting spiders spit at their prey?

11 Assassin bugs are dangerous to humans.
True or false?

12 What causes a firefly to glow?

TINY BUGS

13 How high can a dog flea jump?
a **6in**
b **12in**
c **18in**

14 What do honey ants secrete?

15 The weevil is a vegetarian.
True or false?

16 What's the best defence against the streptococcus bug?

17 How long do most mayflies live?

18 Termites will eat dead members of their own colony.
True or false?

BODY BUGS

19 What should you do if you catch flu?
a **Run around to keep warm**
b **Carry on as usual**
c **Go to bed and drink lots of water**

20 What do mangrove worms taste like?

21 You can remove all dust mites from your carpet by vacuuming them.
True or false?

22 How long can a
tapeworm grow to?
  a 1 yard
  b 4 yards
  c 9 yards

23 How many legs does a
louse have?

24 What disease does the
tsetse fly carry?

BIG BUGS

25 Which movie starred a
big bug called Edgar?

26 In which part of the
world would you find a
10in long praying
mantis?
  a Singapore
  b Sri Lanka
  c Senegal

27 What's the easy
way to distinguish
between a hornet
and a wasp?

28 Tarantulas get their
name from a town in
which country?

29 Who had a close
encounter with a space
slug in the Empire
Strikes Back?

30 Stick insects are experts
at camouflage.
  True or false?

124

FLYING BUGS

31 What is the emperor moth's clever defense?

32 How many times a second can a fly beat its wings?
a **10**
b **200**
c **300**

33 What's a red admiral's favorite snack as a caterpillar?
a **stinging nettles**
b **buttercups**
c **cowslip**

34 Damsel and dragonflies have been around for 400 million years. **True or false?**

35 What's the painted lady butterfly also known as?

36 How do the Tuaregs of the Sahara like their locusts served?

BUDDY BUGS

37 What do sacred scarab beetles eat?

38 Which English city did the Beatles come from?

39 Bumble bees live in hives.
True or false?

40 What does a robug look like?

41 Which historical figure was fond of earthworms?
a **Napoleon**
b **Cleopatra**
c **Queen Victoria**

42 What's a silkworm's favorite food?

solutions

1	b	**26**	b
2	The fat-tailed scorpion	**27**	A hornet has a thin waist
3	True	**28**	Italy
4	Venom	**29**	Han Solo
5	a	**30**	True
6	True	**31**	Its eye-spots in its hindwings
7	False. It was Ant Music.		
8	It's their wings vibrating	**32**	b
9	c	**33**	a
10	A strand of silk	**34**	False. It's 300 million years.
11	False		
12	A chemical reaction in its abdomen	**35**	The cosmopolitan.
		36	Fried, with dates
13	b	**37**	Dung
14	Honeydew	**38**	Liverpool.
15	True	**39**	False
16	Antibiotics	**40**	Big mechanical spider.
17	Just a few days	**41**	b
18	True	**42**	Mulberry leaves
19	c		
20	Crab with a hint of wood		
21	False		
22	c		
23	6		
24	Sleeping sickness		
25	Men in Black		

Turn the page for your bug rating...

127

NOW RATE YOURSELF

0 - 12

You really weren't paying attention, were you? Are you sure you read this book? Or did you just pick it up to swat that fly?!

13 - 24

When it comes to bugs, you're not exactly well-informed. You need to go back over your notes and pay more attention. Or cheat more at quizzes.

25 - 36

Mmm, you're well into bugs aren't you? You probably want to study them at college. Beware – you don't want to become a bug bore.

37 - 42

You're either an entomologist or a cheat. Or maybe you're really a bug. In which case, when did you learn to read? And can you PLEASE get back to the hive now?!